Kiddish Yiddish

Jewish Traditions & Culture in Rhyme

By **Barbara Feltquate**

Illustrated by **Tom Post**

To order additional copies of this book, contact:
Xlibris
844-714-8691
www.Xlibris.com
Orders@Xlibris.com

barbarafeltquatebooks.com

Kiddish Yiddish First Edition Publisher
Chris Angermann
Bardolf & Company
Sarasota, FL

Interior Image Credit: Tom Post

Author Photo: Photographer Al Churilla.

ISBN: 978-1-6641-6307-2 (sc)
ISBN: 978-1-6641-6306-5 (hc)
ISBN: 978-1-6641-6305-8 (e)

Print information available on the last page

Rev. date: 05/20/2021

TESTiMONiALS

KIDDISH YIDDISH, Barbara Feltquate's lyrical poems about the Jewish holidays and life in a Jewish home brought back fond memories of my own childhood, memories that can only be re-created when a child sits on the knee of a grandparent or a parent and learns about the stories that go along with each word of our Yiddish vocabulary.

— Rabbi Steven J. Rubenstein
Temple B'nai Abraham, Beverly, Massachusetts

KIDDISH YIDDISH is Judaism lovingly passed on from a grandparent to grandchildren. Reading it with your loved ones will act as a springboard for further discussion on Judaism and your life and values. I especially love how the illustrations add to the thoughtful poetry.

— Cantor Marsi Vitkus
Jewish Center of Venice, Venice, Florida

KIDDISH YIDDISH is a playful, short, yet meaningful vocabulary of the Jewish faith which will entertain not only the "kids", but their families as well. The word selection has been carefully designed to offer a taste of the beauty and joy of Jewish life.

— Rabbi Arthur I. Baseman
Temple B'nai Israel, Clearwater, Florida

DEDICATION

To my grandchildren
Brad, Alex, Ethan and Jakob
My greatest inspiration

Other books by Barbara Feltquate

Kiddish Yiddish-original publication 2008
Silhouettes of Life
My Italian Heritage
A Hanukkah Miracle
Coming Soon:

Be kind to the Environment
A Children's Primer in Rhyme

Throughout this book
(Y) refers to words of Yiddish origin
(H) refers to words of Hebrew origin
The pronunciation keys use words familiar
to children that approximate the
sound as closely as possible. The stressed syllables are capitalized.
The Hebrew "Ch," which is the sound made trying to clear a popcorn husk
from one's throat, is indicated as "Kh."

THE FAMILY

In Kiddish Yiddish, I follow the more traditional family, made up of Bubbe, Zayde, Mother, Father, Sister and Brother, but mindful and appreciative of all families whether nuclear, extended, single parent, grandparenting, same sex, step, biracial or intermarriage. Raising a family is a sacred duty, where your loved ones inspire you to be the best person you can be. My focus is to describe Jewish traditions and culture in a playful and informative manner and to encourage the telling and discussion of stories representing your own family lore.

BAGEL

(Y) (BAY-gull)

A chewy roll shaped like a ring,
It truly is a mouth-watering thing.
Topped with cream cheese and lox,
Bring it home in a bag or a box!
Originally just a Jewish treat,
Now a yummy food for all to eat.

ZAYDE

(Y) (ZAY-dee)

My grandfather answers
to the name Zayde.
I laugh out loud when I
bounce on his knee.
He takes me to Temple,
teaches me to pray,
Wraps me in his prayer
shawl in a loving way.
We stroll in the park and
see fish in the lake,
Then stop at the bakery
of chocolate cake.

YIDDISH

(Y) (YID-ish)

Yiddish is called the "Mother Tongue."
Bubbe and Zayde spoke it with everyone.
We trace it back for hundreds of years
Through happy times and times of tears.
Today the language is spoken by only a few
But we still claim it proudly as a Jew.

BUBBE

(Y) (BUB-bee)

In Yiddish, my grandmother is called Bubbe.
She bakes cakes and Mandel Bread just for me.
She tells me stories of days gone by
And hugs me tenderly with a sigh.

SHABBAT

(H) (sha-BAHT)

G-D created the world in six days
And gave us the seventh to rest and play.
On Friday when the sun starts to set,
We receive the best present we can get.
Mama lights the candles and prayer is said;
We bless the wine and challah bread,
Share food with friends and family
And thank G-D for His generosity.

CHALLAH

(H) (KHA-la)

We eat challah bread on Friday night
To celebrate Shabbat by candle light.
Years ago, Bubbe
lovingly braided each bread.
Our bellies were full,
happy thoughts in our head.
Today, Mama buys the bread at the store.
It's not quite as good, but we still ask for more.

KIDDUSH

(H) (KEE-doosh)

A prayer we say over a cup of wine
Thankful to G-D for the fruit of the vine.
In Jewish life, we bless many things,
Grateful for all the gifts that G-D brings.

SHAVUOT

(H) (shah-VOO-ot)

This day is important, do you know why?
G-D gave us the Torah at Mount Sinai.
We exchanged an oath with G-D that day
To live our lives in a worthy way.

TORAH

(H) (TOE-rah)

A scroll of all Jewish Law and tradition,
Our history passed down without omission.
It tells of miracles and G-D's loving hand
Helping us find the Promised Land.
It takes a year to read from beginning to end.
When we are finished, we start all over again.

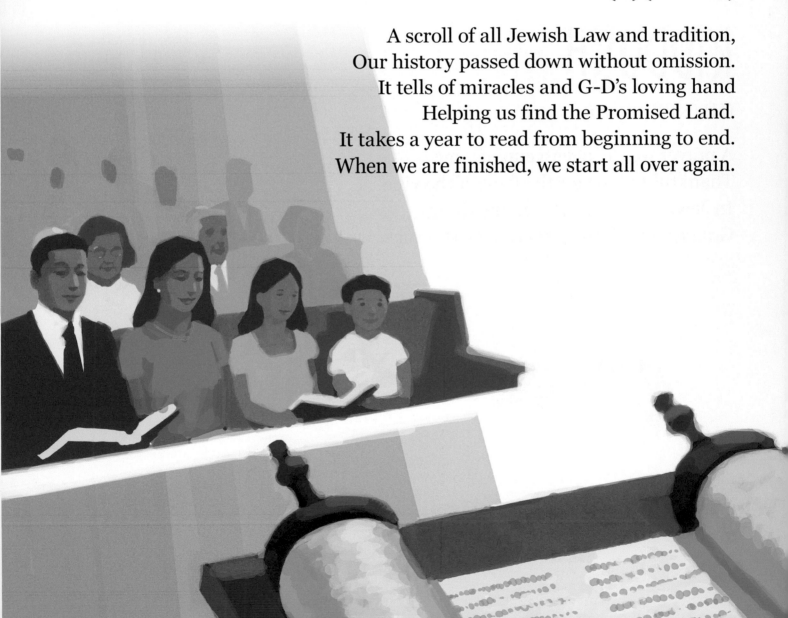

MAGEN DAViD
STAR OF DAViD

(H) (MAH-gain DA-veed)

Two triangles form a six pointed star.
It shines brightly and
guides us wherever we are.
According to legend,
between each small peak
Nestles the world's wisdom,
short and sweet.

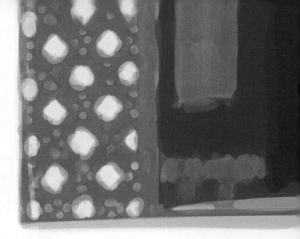

T'FILAH

(H) (te-FEE-lah)

Prayer is a conversation between G-D and you:
You speak from your heart as a caring Jew.
We ask G-D to protect those that we love.
G-D smiles on us from the heavens above.

RABBI

(H) (RAB-bye)

A scholar with a special mission
Who teaches Jewish law and tradition.
A Rabbi's greatest pleasure and joy
Is sharing our heritage
with each girl and boy.

SHUL
SYNAGOGUE
(Y) (shool)

A gathering place to meet and pray
Where people can study and worship all day.
It's the center of the Jewish community
Where G-D is close to you and me.

HAZAN
CANTOR
(H) (khah-zan)

A cantor's voice is blessed from above
For singing and chanting prayers of love
And filling the whole congregation
With joyful sounds and inspiration.

ROSH HASHANAH

(H) (rosh-ha-SHA-na)

When the Jewish New Year starts,
We begin the process to cleanse our hearts.
Looking back at the old year, forward to the new
Mindful to become a better Jew.

SHOFAR

(H) (SHOW-far)

One of the oldest instruments known to man
Made from the hollowed horn of a ram.
Many loud blasts from the horn
"Awaken the listener" on Rosh Hashanah morn.
On Yom Kippur when the sun goes down.
It wails again in a forceful sound

YOM KIPPUR

(H) (YOM-kee-poor)

On this our year's most solemn day
We go to Temple to think and pray.
Grownups fast, which means they don't eat.
Kids try, but it's a difficult feat.
We think about the times we were naughty
And G-D forgives us if we're truly sorry.
With joy and goodness in our heart
We get ready for a brand-new start.

SUKKOT

(H) (SOO-coat)

For forty years our people roamed
Seeking a land, our promised home.
We remember those difficult times
By building a hut of fruits and vines,
A roofless dwelling with the stars above,
To celebrate G-D's bounty and love.

SIMCHAT TORAH

(H) (SIM-khat-TOE-rah)

A year of Torah reading is done
On the last day of Sukkot, let's have fun
March through the Temple cheerfully,
Clap our hands and shout with glee,
Carry scrolls and flags with apples on top
And sing and dance until we drop.

HANUKKAH

(H) (HUN-noo-kah)

On the holiday called the "Miracle of Lights"
We play dreidel and receive gifts each night.
We celebrate our ancestors, the Maccabees,
Who took back the temple and set Jerusalem free.
With only enough oil to burn one day
They needed G-D and began to pray.
He heard their prayers, and we're still amazed
How oil for one night lasted eight days.

MENORAH

(H) (meh-NO-ra)

The candelabra used on Sabbath night
Has seven candles that shine bright.
The special holder at Hanukkah time
Has two more, which makes nine:
One to light the other eight,
Honoring the miracle we celebrate.

GELT

(Y) (gehlt)

Hanukkah chocolate money's called gelt.
We eat it quickly before it can melt.
It adds to the spirit of the holiday
If we share and give some of it away.

DREIDEL

(Y) (DRAY-dil)

At Hanukkah we play with a top that spins.
Its letters gimmel, hey, nun and shin
Spell a message that we share:
"A great miracle happened there."
Twirl it quickly and wait till it stops
You may win gelt or candy drops.

PURIM

(H) (POO-rim)

We honor Queen Esther for being brave
When Haman caused harm and misbehaved.
She saved the Jew from certain doom
And now we dance around the room,
Shake rattles and stomp our feet
To rejoice in evil Haman's defeat.
We wear colorful costumes, put on plays,
Feast and celebrate happy days.

HAMANTASHEN

(Y) (HA-mahn-tash-in)

A pastry and favorite Purim treat,
Stuffed with poppy seeds, yummy to eat,
Shaped like bad Haman's hat or ear.
Take three bites and it will disappear.

PASSOVER

PESACH
(H)(PAY-saach)

Around the Seder table we tell the story
Of Moses leading us from slavery to glory.
He said to Egypt's King, "Let my people go!"
G-D sent ten plagues when Pharaoh said, "No!"
And later helped by parting the Red Sea
And took us to Canaan where we became free.

SEDER

(H) (SAY-dur)

With family and friends we hold dear
We gather for a special meal every year
To renew our memory of the Exodus
With stories and symbols important to us.
We eat matzah, which is unleavened bread,
And drink some wine that may go to our head.
It's fun to sing the Passover songs,
Especially when everyone sings along.

SEDER PLATE

Six special foods on a beautiful plate
Tell the story of our people's fate.
Salted water and dipping green
Suggest tears and a springtime scene.
A Passover offering with a lamb's leg,
Hope for the future in a roasted egg,
Something bitter, something sweet,
From slavery to freedom,
a miraculous feat!

AFIKOMAN

(H) (ah-fee-KO-mun)

Finding the Afikoman is the last quest
It's the part children like the best
Zayde hides matzah while we close our eyes.
When we find out where, we win a prize.

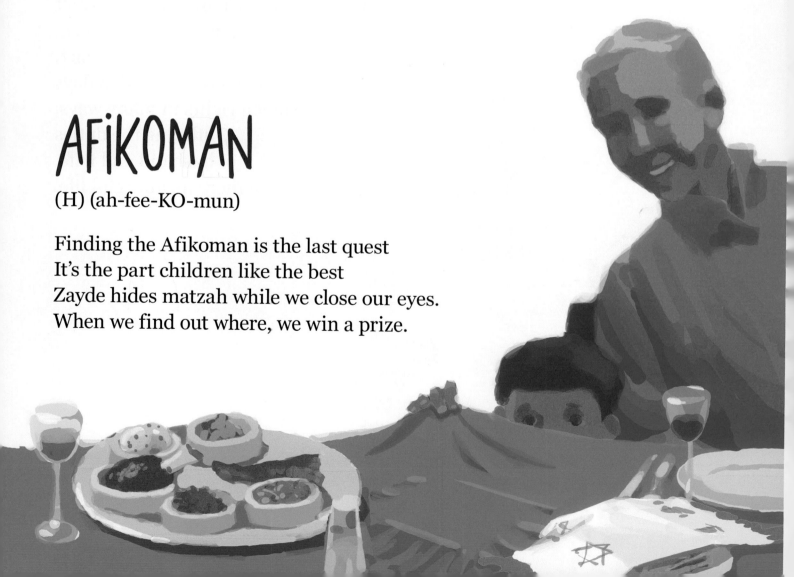

CHUPPAH

(Y) (KHOO-pa)

Under an open, tent-like canopy
The Rabbi performs the wedding ceremony
Symbolizing the home of husband and wife
Where they will live a good and happy life.

KETUBAH

(H) (Keh-TOO-baa)

The ancient Jewish marriage contract
Is surprisingly modern,
and that's a fact.
Even back in olden days
It gave women rights in many ways,
Outlining the duties
of husband and wife,
To make for a more meaningful life.

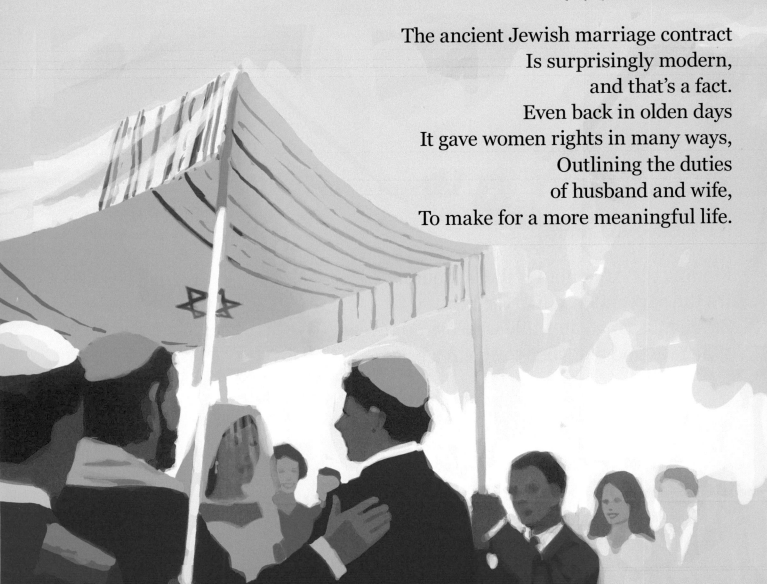

MEZUZAH

(H) (meh-ZOO-zah)

Attached to our home's doorpost
To protect and bless those we love most
On parchment no bigger than a pin,
A tiny scroll rests snuggly within.
Its Torah passages clearly say
To love G-D and follow His way

KOSHER

(H) (KO-sher)

If you prepare meals fried, baked or raw
By following old Jewish dietary law,
You must take very special care
To use separate dishes and silverware.
Do not mix foods like milk and meat.
Good news, you can eat almost anything sweet.

MITZVAH

(H) (MITZ-vaa)

Do a kind and thoughtful deed,
Help someone, fulfill a need.
It won't matter what time of day
You'll please G-D in every way.

TZEDAKAH

(H) (tseh-da-kaa)

G-D bestows many blessings on you.
You return them by being a generous Jew.
Each has a duty to give of himself
An act of giving is better than wealth.

BAR/BAT MITZVAH

SON/DAUGHTER
OF COMMANDMENT
(H) (bat/baht-MITZ-vaa)

Our heritage celebrates coming of age.
At thirteen, you enter a responsible stage.
You get to take part in the prayer service.
I know it sounds scary, but don't be nervous.
Your Hebrew lessons will be helpful to you
As you start your life as a devoted Jew.

TALLiT

(H) (TAH-leet)

A fringed four cornered prayer shawl
Fits nicely on shoulders big or small.
This silky cloth plays a special part
When it touches the Torah,
it kisses your heart.

YARMULKE

(Y) (YAR-mull-KAH)
KIPPAH
(H) (KI-pah)

The small, round head covering
Reminds us G-D is above everything.
Wear it all day or just at Temple.
It shows respect plain and simple.

MAZEL TOV

(H/Y) (MA-zell-tov)

Raise your glass to make a toast,
What is the saying said the most?
"Mazel Tov!!"
When a new baby joins a family,
What do you say to show your glee?
"Mazel Tov!!"
It's a Hebrew and Yiddish word,
The most cheerful expression
you ever heard.
It means I am very happy for you,
Good luck, and congratulation, too.

SHALOM

(H) (shah-LOM)

A Hebrew word that means "live in peace."
If everyone practiced it, all wars would cease.
It's a friendly word to say both hello and goodbye.
We don't get confused and I can't explain why.
But there's one thing I am certain of:
When you say it, you are bestowing love.

ACKNOWLEDGMENTS

There are many people that have helped make KIDDISH YIDDISH a reality, and I thank you all. Special thanks to my wonderful husband Harvey for his love and support. To my sister Janet Miller, who came up with the title, and with her husband Rick, contributed knowledge of Jewish rituals and culture, as well as pronunciation guides. To Norm and Toni Steinberg who supported me throughout the process. To special friends, Joan, Pam, Shirley, Faye, and Mary for their steadfast enthusiasm and support. To my children Debbie and David and their respective spouses Glenn Maller and Anne Feltquate for their ongoing encouragement. To my mother Ethel Amato, posthumously, who read everything I wrote and always encouraged me with her simple, down-to-earth advice. I still hear your words and know you watch over me. A special thank you to Ron Eckert for his insight on the new vertical layout. I also wish to express my gratitude to the various clergy who read the manuscript and kindly wrote testimonials.

About The Book

From Bagel to Shalom, this children's glossary of Jewish words in rhyme follows three generations of a family through a year of holidays, rituals and traditions. Poems and illustrations tell stories in the loving way grandparents share memories with their offspring, while encouraging further discussion about the rich contribution of Hebrew and Yiddish to our language and society. Ideal for parents, grandparents, teachers, and librarians that take pleasure in reading with children and exploring the ABC's of Jewish culture in an evocative, fun-filled way.

The Author

Barbara Feltquate has always had a passion for poetry and storytelling. The birth of her four grandsons got her thinking about all the wonderful memories her grandparents shared with her when she was young. She realized the importance of sharing those special memories and creating new memories with her grandchildren. The result, Kiddish Yiddish, is her first book; a celebration of the culture and traditions of her Jewish heritage. Barbara and her husband Harvey now divide their time between Cape Cod, Massachusetts and Venice, Florida, where she is at work on her next children's book-in rhyme, of course.

The Illustrator

Tom Post's love for art goes back to his earliest childhood memories, drawing inspiration from the Sunday comics. By 17 he was creating 17 foot window paintings for the local movie theatres advertising their feature films. He has a BFA in fine arts from the Columbus College of Art and Design and has been a freelance illustrator/ portrait artist since 1987. He resides in Cincinnati, Ohio with his high school sweet heart, Ann and their two beautiful children.

Please visit his website, tompost.studio and follow him on instagram, tompostart to see his latest art.

Printed in the United States
by Baker & Taylor Publisher Services